A Grandmother
Is God's Blessing

To Granny

From Chris and Mandy 5/96

Copyright © 1995 by Garborg's Heart 'n Home, Inc.
Published by Garborg's Heart 'n Home, Inc., P.O. Box 20132, Bloomington, MN 55420

Illustrations © 1995 by Stephen Whittle.
All rights reserved.
ISBN 1-881830-18-7

A loving grandmother is beyond price; there is no measuring of her goodness.

*T*he human heart, at whatever age, opens to the heart that opens in return.

MARIA EDGEWORTH

$\mathcal{A}$ child's hand in yours—
what tenderness and power
it arouses. You are instantly
the very touchstone of
wisdom and strength.

MARJORIE HOLMES

$\mathcal{I}$ love these little people; and it is not a slight
thing when they, who are so fresh from God, love us.

CHARLES DICKENS

The child should be taught from the very first that the whole world is his world, that adult and child share one world, that all generations are needed.

PEARL S. BUCK

Your goodness and unfailing kindness shall be with me all of my life.

PSALM 23:6 TLB

A grandmother has
ears that truly listen,
arms that always hold.
She has a love that's never-ending
and a heart of purest gold.

$\mathcal{W}$e should all have one person
who knows how to bless us despite
the evidence. Grandmother was that
person to me.

PHYLLIS THEROUX

$\mathcal{P}$raise the children
and they will blossom.

IRISH PROVERB

$\mathcal{G}$randmothers...can be invaluable to the world of little people. In today's world, they are often the only grownups who have time.

DR. JAMES DOBSON

$\mathcal{P}$ut on a heart of compassion, kindness, humility, gentleness, and patience.

COLOSSIANS 3:12 NAS

*I*f wrinkles must be written on our brows, let them not be written upon the heart. The spirit should not grow old.

JAMES A. GARFIELD

*T*hose who love deeply never grow old.

SIR ARTHUR WING PINERO

*W*e turn not older with years, but newer every day.

EMILY DICKINSON

Grandparents are very special,
they are friends of treasured worth...
and one who knows their love
has the greatest gift on earth.

*G*ive a little love to a child
and you get a great deal back.

JOHN RUSKIN

*N*ow that I've reached the age,
or maybe the stage, where I need
my children more than they need
me, I really understand
how grand it is to
be a grandmother.

MARGARET WHITLAM

*L*et the children come
to me, for the kingdom
of God belongs to
such as they.

MARK 10:14 TLB

*B*lessed be childhood which brings down
something of heaven into the midst of
our...earthliness.

HENRI FRÉDÉRIC AMIEL

*C*heerfulness is the atmosphere
in which all things thrive.

JEAN PAUL RICHTER

*G*randparents have a toleration
for and a patience with the boys
and girls that parents lack.

MARGARET E. SANGSTER

*P*atience is the
companion of wisdom.

ST. AUGUSTINE

$\mathcal{T}$he more miles you have on you
from the travels of the heart, the more
simple and childlike your faith becomes.

GLORIA GAITHER

$\mathcal{M}$ost of all, let love guide your life.

COLOSSIANS 3:14 TLB

$\mathcal{S}$o many things we love are you...
flowers and beautiful handmade
things—small stitches. So much of
our reading and thinking, so many
sweet customs.... It is all you...
dear Grandma.

ANNE MORROW LINDBERGH

If you laugh a lot, when you get older your wrinkles will be in the right places.

ANDREW MASON

It is a fine seasoning for joy to think of those we love.

MOLIÈRE

*W*rinkles should merely indicate where smiles have been.

MARK TWAIN

$\mathcal{A}$ cheerful heart has a continual feast.

PROVERBS 15:15 NRSV

$\mathcal{C}$heerfulness and contentment are great beautifiers, and are famous preservers of good looks.

CHARLES DICKENS

*S*ay only what is
good and helpful to those you are
talking to, and what will give them
a blessing.

EPHESIANS 4:29 TLB

A grandmother is someone who prays
for us, listens to us, and lends us a
comforting hand and an
understanding ear.

$\mathcal{H}$appy is [she] who knows what to remember of the past, what to enjoy in the present, and what to plan for the future.

A. GLASON

$\mathcal{I}$n youth we learn; in age we understand.

MARIE VON EBNER-ESCHENBACH

*G*od gave us memories
so that we might have
roses in December.

SIR JAMES M. BARRIE

*T*he head learns new things, but the heart
forevermore practices old experiences.

HENRY WARD BEECHER

I shall grow old, but never lose
life's zest,
Because the road's last turn will be
the best.

HENRY VAN DYKE

*B*lessed is the influence
of one true, loving human
soul on another.

GEORGE ELIOT

A Wish

*H*ealth to enjoy the blessings sent
From Heaven; a mind unclouded, strong;
A cheerful heart; a wise content;
An honored age; and song.

HORACE

But the wisdom that comes from heaven is first of all pure and full of quiet gentleness.

JAMES 3:17 TLB

It is as grandmothers that our mothers come into the fullness of their grace.

CHRISTOPHER MORLEY

*I*f a child is to keep his inborn sense of wonder...he needs the companionship of at least one adult who can share it, rediscovering with him the joy, excitement, and mystery of the world we live in.

RACHEL CARSON

*T*he greatest use of life is to spend it for something that will outlast it.

WILLIAM JAMES

*S*ee to it that you really do love each other warmly, with all your hearts.

1 PETER 1:22 TLB

$\mathcal{W}$e live in the present, we dream of the future, but we learn eternal truths from the past. Isn't it splendid to think of all the things there are to find out about?

LUCY MAUD MONTGOMERY

*H*uman love and the delights of friendship, out of which are built the memories that endure, are also to be treasured up as hints of what shall be hereafter.

BEDE JARRETT

There is a fountain of youth: it is your mind, your talents, the creativity you bring to your life and the lives of people you love.

SOPHIA LOREN

A joyful heart is life itself, and rejoicing lengthens one's life.

ECCLESIASTICUS

The hearts that love will
Know never winter's frost and chill,
Summer's warmth is in them still.

<small>EBEN EUGENE REXFORD</small>

God is love, and those who
abide in love abide in God,
and God abides in them.

<small>1 JOHN 4:16 NRSV</small>

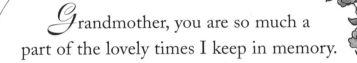

*G*randmother, you are so much a
part of the lovely times I keep in memory.

I cease not to give thanks for you,
making mention of you in my prayers.

<small>EPHESIANS 1:16 KJV</small>

*C*ease to inquire whatever the future has in store, and take as a gift whatever the day brings forth.

HORACE

I will never leave you or forsake you.

HEBREWS 13:5 NRSV

$\mathcal{T}$he future belongs to those who believe in the beauty of their dreams.

ELEANOR ROOSEVELT

$\mathcal{Y}$outh is the time for the adventures of the body, but age for the triumphs of the mind.

LOGAN PEARSALL SMITH

$\mathcal{W}$e find delight in the beauty
and happiness of children that
makes the heart too big for
the body.

RALPH WALDO EMERSON

$\mathcal{C}$hildren are a bridge
to heaven.

PERSIAN PROVERB

$\mathcal{W}$e need time to dream,
time to remember, time to reach
the infinite. Time to be.

GLADYS TABER

$\mathcal{L}$ife is the childhood of immortality.

DANIEL A. POLING

$\mathcal{W}$hat feeling is so nice as
a child's hand in yours? So small,
so soft and warm, like a kitten
huddling in the shelter of your clasp.

MARJORIE HOLMES

$\mathcal{A}$s a father has compassion
for his children, so the
Lord has compassion
for those who fear him.

PSALM 103:13 NRSV

$\mathcal{S}$atisfy us in our earliest youth with your lovingkindness, giving us constant joy to the end of our lives.

PSALM 90:14 TLB

$\mathcal{Y}$outh lasts much longer than young people think.

If becoming a grandmother were only a matter of choice, I should advise every one of you straight away to become one. There is no fun for old people like it!

HANNAH WHITALL SMITH